Understanding My Emotions

When I'm Sad

Understanding My Emotions

When I'm Angry

When I'm Embarrassed

When I'm Happy

When I'm Lonely

When I'm Overwhelmed

When I'm Sad

When I'm Scared

When I'm Sorry

When I'm Surprised

When I'm Worried

Understanding My Emotions

When I'm Sad

ALEXANDRA DALTON

Understanding My Emotions
When I'm Sad

Copyright © 2016 by Village Earth Press, a division of Harding House Publishing. All rights reserved. No part of this publication may be reproduced or transmitted in any form or by any means, electronic or mechanical, including photocopying, recording, taping, or any information storage and retrieval system, without permission from the publisher.

Village Earth Press
Vestal, New York 13850
www.villageearthpress.com

First Printing
9 8 7 6 5 4 3 2 1

Series ISBN (paperback): 978-1-62524-440-6
ISBN (paperback): 978-1-62524-381-2
ebook ISBN: 978-1-62524-137-5
    Library of Congress Control Number: 2014944105

Author: Dalton, Alexandra.

Contents

To the Teacher or Parent	7
When I'm Sad	9
Find Out More	42
Feeling Words	44
Index	46
Picture Credits	47
About the Author	48

To the Teacher or Parent

More than a hundred years ago, John Dewey insisted that the true purpose of schooling was not simply to teach children a trade but to train them in deeper habits of mind. Social-emotional learning builds on Dewey's theory further, suggesting that emotional skills are crucial to both academic performance and future success in life.

The research is definitive: emotional training is good for children! A recent study, reported in the *New York Times*, found that preschoolers who had even a single year of social-emotional training continued to perform better two years after they left the program; they were less aggressive and less anxious than children who hadn't participated in the program. Another study found that K-12 students who received some form of emotional instruction scored an average of 11 percentile points higher on standardized achievement tests. A similar study found a nearly 20 percent decrease in students' violent behaviors.

The goal of this series of books, UNDERSTANDING MY EMOTIONS, is to instill in young children a foundation of emotional intelligence. Use these books to help children learn to understand, identify, and regulate their emotions. Give them important tools that will serve them well for the rest of their lives!

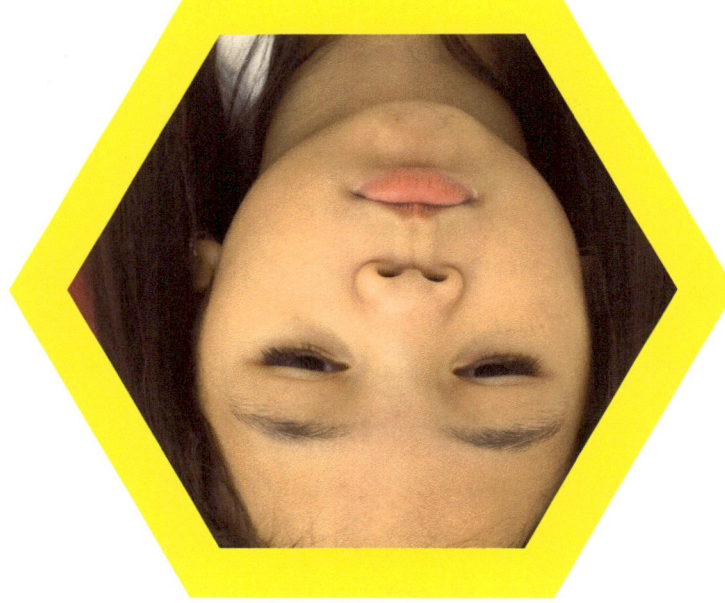

SAD

When I'm

Every single day of my life, I have many, many feelings. You can tell what I'm feeling by looking at my face.

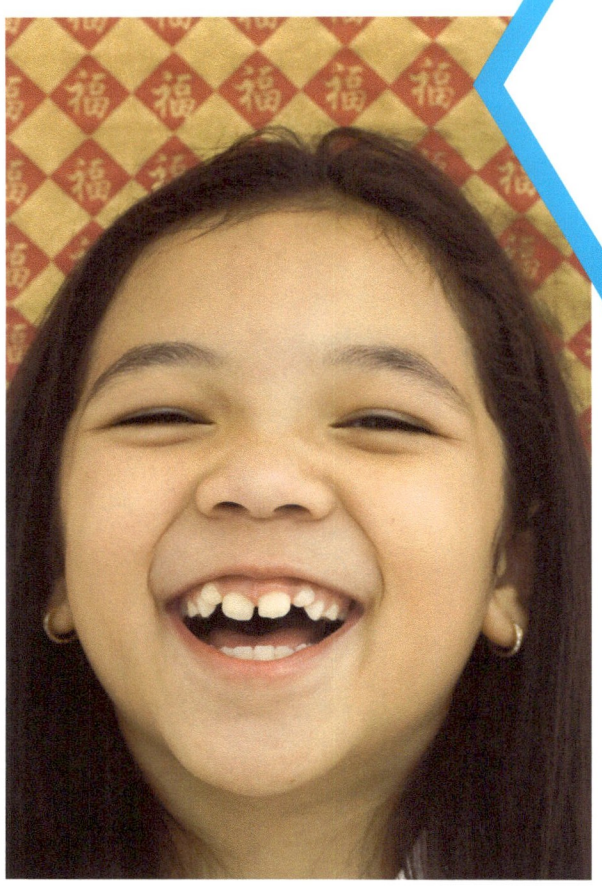

My feelings come and go. I might feel happy at breakfast before I go to school.

At school, I feel proud of the drawing I made of my family.

When I'm eating lunch with my friends at school, I feel silly.

I feel excited after school at my dance class.

I'm filled with loving feelings when I'm with my dad or when I'm petting my dog.

When I'm playing the piano, I get so interested in what I'm doing that I forget about everything else.

I feel REALLY interested when I'm watching a 3D movie.

But other feelings I have aren't fun to feel. They don't feel good. I don't like to feel scared or angry. I don't like feeling shy or embarrassed. I don't like being bored.

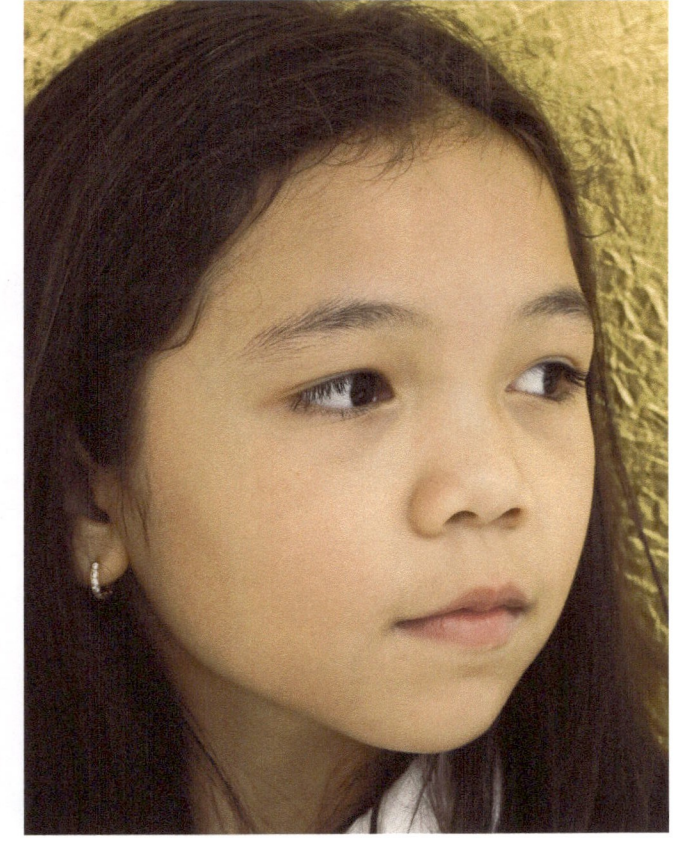

And I really, really don't like feeling sad.

But sad things happen. That's just the way life is. No one feels happy all the time.

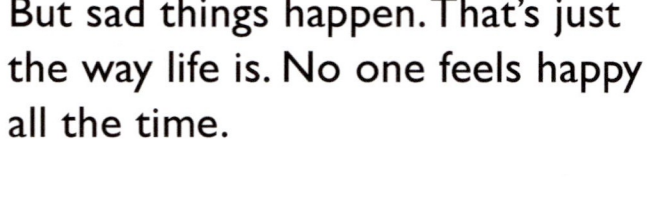

Everyone feels sad sometimes.

Grown-ups get sad too! They feel sad the same way that little people do.

Even my dog feels sad sometimes!

I can tell when people are sad because their faces tell me. Sometimes when people are sad, they look a little like this sad face.

Their mouths look like an upside-down smile.

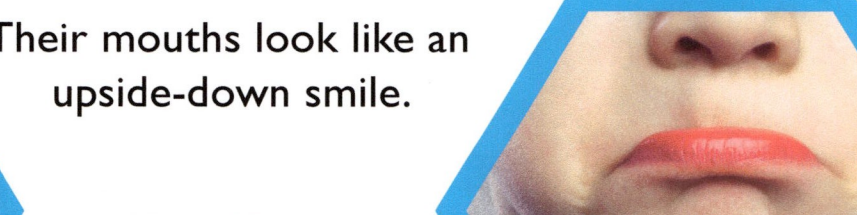

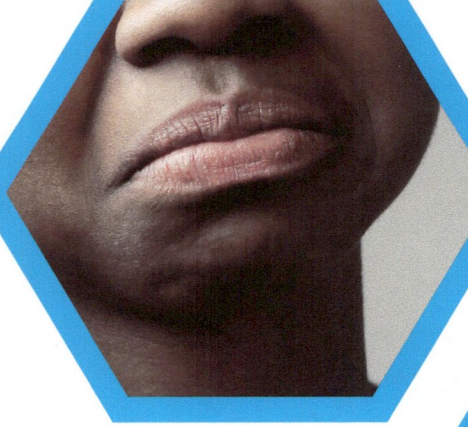

But most of the time when people are feeling sad, they don't really look like a sad face with an upside-down smile.

They might just push their lips together tight.

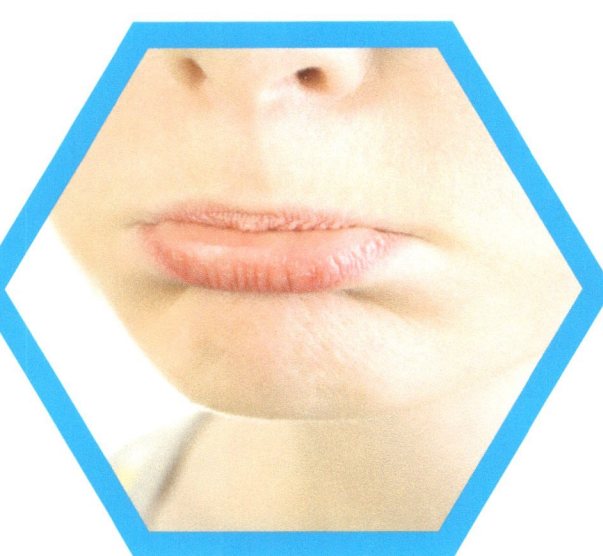

Or they might stick out their bottom lip.

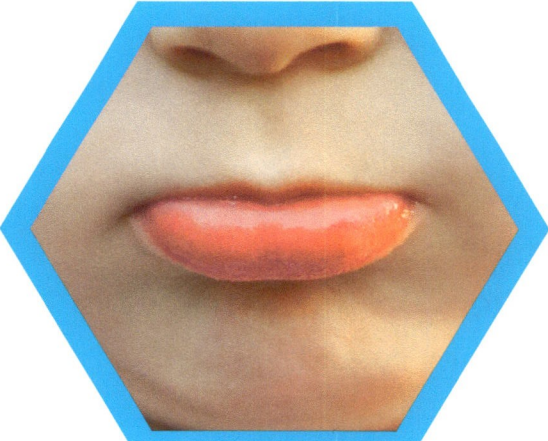
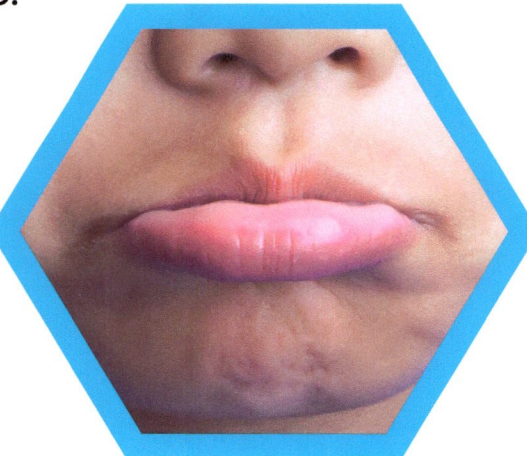

Other parts of a person's face can tell me if that person is sad.

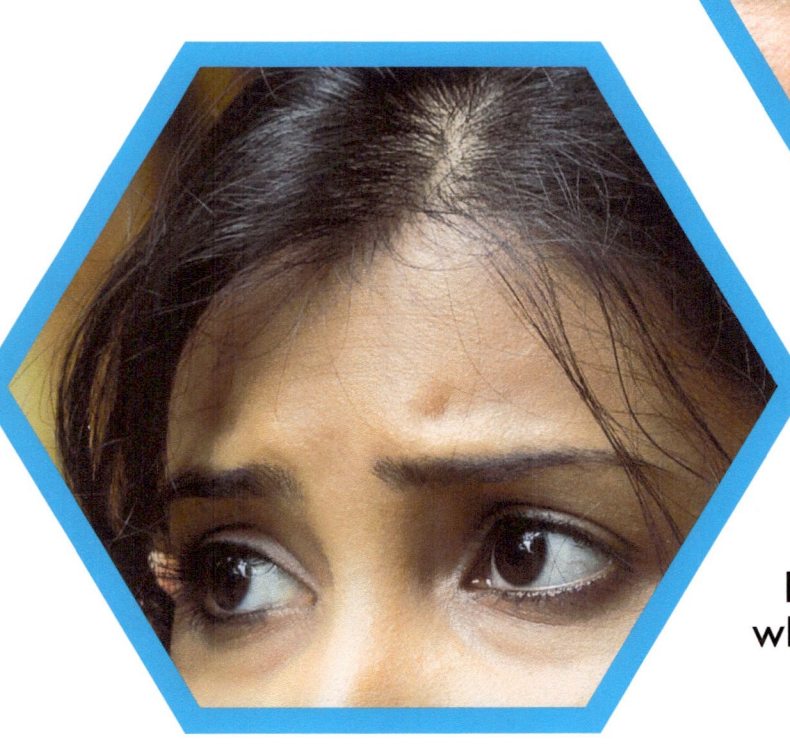

Some people get little puckers on their foreheads when they're sad.

Sometimes when people are sad, their mouths don't turn up or down. Their mouths look like a straight line. They might get really quiet and not want to talk. They may just stare into space thinking sad thoughts.

Sometimes people cry when they're sad.

When people cry hard,
they might squeeze their
eyes shut and open
their mouths
really wide.

Even grown-ups cry sometimes!

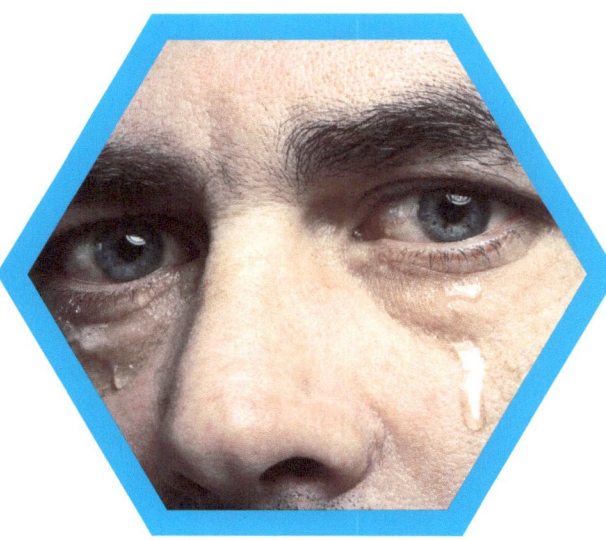

It's not just people's faces that tell me when they're sad. Sometimes their whole bodies say they're sad. They might sit with their shoulders slumped and their heads down.

They might hide their faces in their hands.

Sometimes they hunch up their knees.

All kinds of different things make people feel sad.

My baby sister feels sad when she wants my mom to come home from work.

My big brother felt sad when he didn't get his driver's license.

My friend Jason was sad when we wouldn't let him play with us.

My mom was really, really sad when her friend died. She cried for a long time.

My grandpa was unhappy when he had to move out of his home and live somewhere else. After a few weeks, he was happier.

My dog feels sad when we leave him home. He wishes he could go with us!

A lot of times, being sad is all mixed up with other feelings.

I felt sad and worried when my dog was sick.

I felt sad and disappointed when I didn't get picked to be the Sugar Plum Fairy.

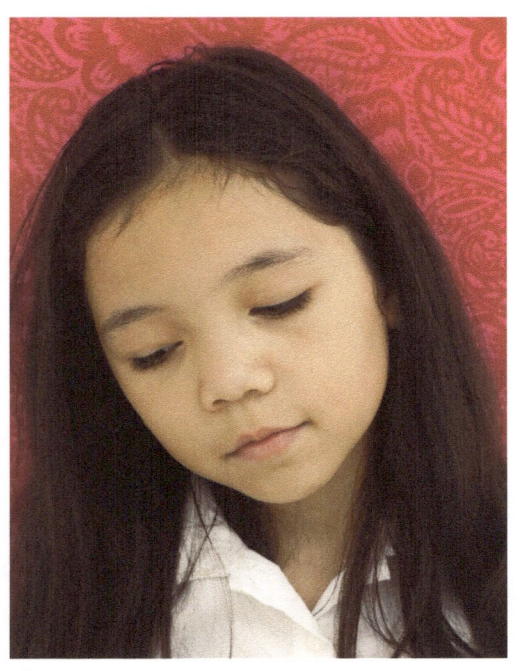

I felt sad after school yesterday because it was too rainy to play outside—and I was bored.

My best friend Lucy is sad because her grandma is sick in the hospital. Lucy's scared her grandma might die. Her scared feelings make her feel sad.

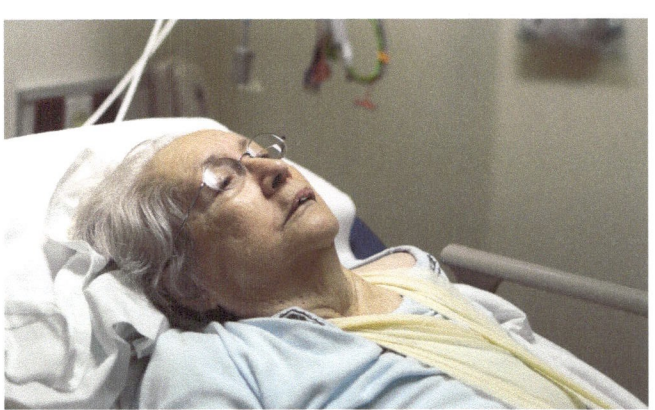

My friend Carlos says he feels sad when his parents scold him—but he feels mad too. His unhappy feelings are all mixed up with mad feelings.

Sometimes things happen that make me sad. Sometimes I'm sad about things I'm scared might happen. Lots of times, other people make me sad, even when they don't mean to. But all those sad, angry, disappointed, scared, worried, bored feelings are inside ME.

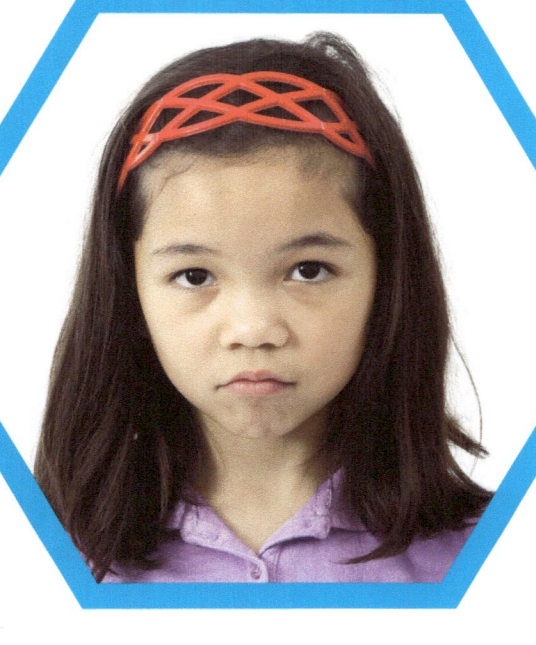

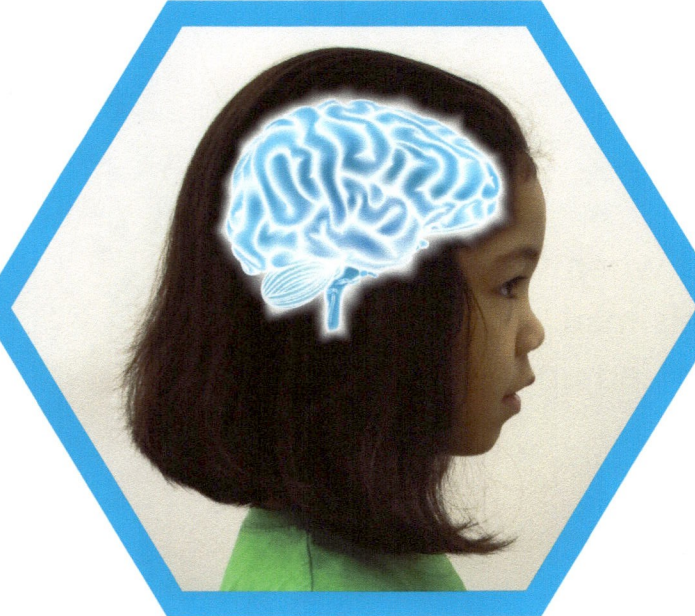

They happen inside my head. They happen in my brain.

This is what my brain looks like. It looks a little like a walnut! But it can do all sorts of amazing things.

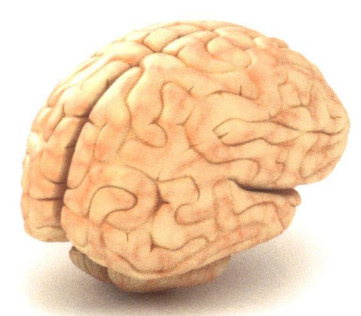

I use my brain every time I have an idea. I use it when I learn, when I play, and when I make things.

My brain is always busy. It even tells my heart to beat. It makes my stomach do its job. It tells my lungs to breathe. It gets messages from my eyes and my ears. It helps me talk, and it tells my arms and legs what to do. My brain is like the boss of my entire body. It sends out messages to every part of me.

My brain is where my sad and happy feelings happen. When I feel scared, it's because of changes inside my brain. When I feel angry, something else is happening inside my brain.

All these feelings inside my brain are called emotions.

Emotions start out inside my brain, but they can change the rest of my body too. When I'm scared, I might get a tummy ache.

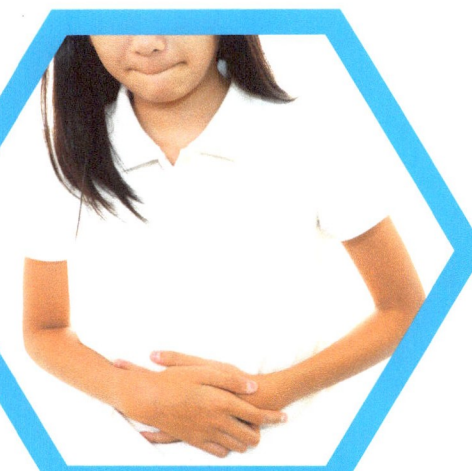

When I feel embarrassed, my face gets red.

And when I'm sad, I might get tears in my eyes. I might feel tired. My head might hurt.

When I scrape my knee, it's my knee that hurts—but I feel sad too.

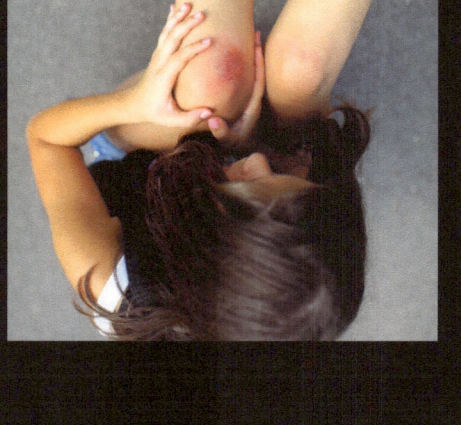

What happens to my body, changes my brain too. When I have a runny nose, my brain might make sad feelings.

That's because my brain and the rest of my body are connected. What happens inside my brain changes the rest of my body. Everything in my body works together.

When something bad happens, my brain makes unhappy feelings. But once in a while, I feel sad for no reason. There's nothing wrong. I just feel unhappy. My dad says I got out of the wrong side of the bed! That's silly. My bed doesn't have a right and a wrong side!

But when I'm tired, sometimes my brain makes sad feelings. If I take a nap, I wake up feeling happier.

When I'm unhappy, there are other things I can do to help the sad feeling go away. If I do something I like doing, my brain might stop making sad feelings.

I might practice my dance moves.

I could call my grandma and tell her about my sad feelings. My grandma is a good listener. She always understands what I'm feeling—and that helps me feel better.

Or I could spend some time with my dad. He almost always makes me laugh.

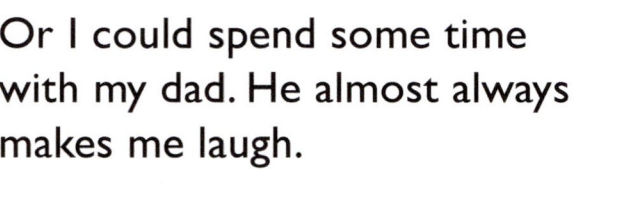

When I'm sad, I feel better when I give my dog a hug.

She licks my face—and pretty soon she makes me smile!

Another thing that gives me happy feelings is helping someone else. When I do something nice for someone, it makes me feel happy.

One time I was sad because my computer was broke. Then I decided to go visit my grandma. I brought her a plant to put in her window. I forgot about being sad.

I made my grandma smile too.

It's okay to feel sad. Everyone feels bad when sad things happen. But the unhappy feelings won't last forever. Sometimes just putting a smile on my face makes me feel better. Smiles make happy feelings!

Find Out More

You can learn more about your emotions by going online and checking out these websites. Some of the sites have videos you can watch or games you can play. You could also read the other books in this series to find out more about feelings—or you could go to your library and see if you can find the books listed on the next page. There's a lot more you can learn about sadness and other feelings!

On the Internet

It's My Life: Emotions
pbskids.org/itsmylife/emotions

KidsHealth: Feelings
kidshealth.org/kid/feeling

Model Me: Faces and Emotions
www.modelmekids.com/emotions_dvd.html

Why Am I So Sad?
kidshealth.org/kid/feeling/thought/sadness.html

In Books

Aliki. *Feelings*. New York: Greenwillow Books, 2007.

Cosson, M. J. *The Smart Kid's Guide to Feeling Sad or Angry*. North Mankato, MN: Childs World, 2014.

Greive, Andrew Trevor. *The Blue Day Book for Kids: A Lesson in Cheering Yourself Up*. Kansas City, MO: Andrews McMeel, 2005.

Mundy, Michaelene. *Sad Isn't Bad: A Good-Grief Guidebook for Kids Dealing with Loss*. St. Meinrad, IN: Abbey Press, 2014.

Krueger, David. *What Is a Feeling?* Seattle, WA: Parenting Press, 2013.

Rotner, Shelley. *Lots of Feelings*. Minneapolis, MN: Millbrook Press, 2003.

Snow, Todd. *Feelings to Share from A to Z*. Lake Elmo, MN: Maren Green, 2007.

Feeling Words

Sad is just one of the words we use when we talk about feelings. There are many more words that describe feelings. Here are some of those words.

Excited

Scared

Embarrassed

Worried

Guilty

Hurt

Proud

Lonely

Shy

Sorry

Surprised

Bored

Index

An index is a way you can quickly find something inside a book. The numbers tell you exactly what page to go to if you want to find that word.

angry 14, 32, 34, 43
arms 33

bed 37
bored 14, 30, 32, 45
brain 32–38
brother 28

cry 24–25

dad 12, 37–38
dance 11, 38
disappointed 30, 32
dog 12, 19, 29–30, 39
drawing 10

ears 33
embarrassed 14, 35, 44
excited 11, 44
eyes 24, 33, 35

family 10
foreheads 22
friend 28–29, 31

grandma 31, 38, 40
grandpa 29
grown-ups 18, 25

hands 27
happy 10, 16, 34, 40–41
heart 33

legs 33
lips 21
loving 12
lungs 33

mad 31
mom 28–29

nap 37

parents 31
piano 13
play 28, 30, 33, 42
proud 10, 45

runny nose 36

scared 14, 31–32, 34–35, 44

school 10–11, 30
shoulders 26
shy 14, 45
sick 30–31
silly 11, 37
sister 28
smile 20–21, 39–41
stomach 33

tears 35
thoughts 23
tired 35, 37
tummy ache 35

worried 30, 32, 44

Picture Credits

p. 9: Jesse Kunerth
p. 10: Jesse Kunerth
p. 11: Jesse Kunerth
p. 12: Jesse Kunerth
p. 13: Jesse Kunerth
p. 14: Jesse Kunerth
p. 15: Jesse Kunerth
p. 16: Belinda Pretorius, Fasphotographic, Zhangyang, Wavebreak Media
p. 17: Vinicius Tupinamba, 2xSamara.com, Patrick Foto, Auremar
p. 18: Ollyy
p. 19: Valentin Creciun
p. 20: Lack-O-Keen, Eldar Nurkovic, Ollyy, Taramara78
p. 21: Alexander Orlov, Kitisak Pingkasarn, Ana Blazic Pavlovic
p. 22: A & N Photography, Ollyy
p. 23: NeydtStock, Fototaras, Laurin Rinder
p. 24: Blacqkbook, Lane V. Erickson, Dr322, Hanna Mariah, Parinyabinsuk
p. 25: Aastock, Artem Furman, Laurin Rinder, Howard Klaaste
p. 26: Alexandre Nunes, Jochen Schoenfeld, rmnoa357
p. 27: Anna Jurkovska, Sabfoto, IC Snaps, Andrei Shumskiy
p. 28: Paul Hakimata Photography, Patrick Foto, Art Casta
p. 29: Joseph, Diego Cervo, Eric Isselee
p. 30: Jesse Kunerth
p. 31: Fotoluminate LLC, Patrick Foto, Emese
p. 32: Jesse Kunerth, Christos Georghiou
p. 33: Vladgrin, Alex Mit, Mopic
p. 34: Fabio Berti, Andromina
p. 35: Sunabesyou, Jesse Kunerth
p. 36: Sebastian Kaulitzki, Tom Wang, Melianiaka Kanstantsin
p. 37: Photobac, Jesse Kunerth
p. 38: Jesse Kunerth, Leungchopan
p. 39: Jesse Kunerth
p. 40: Jesse Kunerth
p. 41: Jesse Kunerth
p. 44: Fotolia: © Fasphotographic, © Cantor Pannato, © Andres Rodriguez, © Gabriel Blaj, © Moodboard Premium, © Halfpoint
p. 45: Fotolia: © Cantor Pannato, © Blend Images, © Zhekos, © Olly, © Wavebreak Media Micro; © Serrnovik | Dreamstime.com

About the Author

Alexandra Dalton was a teacher, and now she is a writer. When she was a teacher, she helped her students talk about their feelings. She knows that it's hard work sometimes to talk about our feelings—but she knows we feel better and we get along with each other better when we can use our words to talk about how we feel. Alexandra has three children. She also has a dog and a cat and four goats. She lives in New York State.